BBC Children's Books
Published by the Penguin Group
Penguin Books Ltd, 80 Strand, London WC2R 0RL, England
Penguin Group (Australia) Ltd, 250 Camberwell Road,
Camberwell, Victoria 3124, Australia (a division of Pearson
Australia Group Pty Ltd)
Canada, India, New Zealand, South Africa

Published by BBC Children's Books, 2008
Text and design © Children's Character Books, 2008

10 9 8 7 6 5 4 3 2 1

Written by Mark Hillsdon
Designed by Dan Newman/Perfect Bound Ltd

BBC and Top Gear (word marks and logos) are trademarks
of the British Broadcasting Corporation and used under
license.
Top Gear © 2005
BBC Logo™ & © BBC 1996.
All rights reserved

ISBN: 978-1-40590-459-9
Printed in China

It's no **wonder** Michael Schumacher has retired. He's slower than **me!**

Contents

I could say **Maserati** before I could say **Mummy!**

The new **fastest** car and you **didn't** like it!

Well, speed isn't **everything.** I can't believe I just said that!

Introduction

Welcome to Top Gear Supercars!

Welcome to Top Gear Supercars! Porsche, Lamborghini, Maserati, Bugatti, to name just a few. Jeremy will clamber behind the wheel of them all of these before you can even *begin* to utter the word 'Power'.

Then the Stig will push these supercars to their limits to see just exactly how much power it takes to make it to the top of the power lap board (it's 625bhp, by the way).

Richard drools over the Lamborghini Reventon and even James sees if he could take a Bugatti Veyron over the 250mph mark. And surprisingly, he does.

So what is it about these sleek speed demons (the cars, not Jeremy, Richard and James) that makes grown men drop to their knees and pray for a lotto win?

Well, here are a few reasons for starters...

1. They're fast. Very fast. Most will easily break the 200mph mark.
2. They're rare. Usually just a handful are made and then sold to very rich people who selfishly stash them away in private collections.
3. They're road cars, not racing cars, so 'anyone' (ie, the filthy rich) can drive them. One of the key tests on Top Gear is that they can make it over a speed bump and not do any damage to the precious bodywork.
4. Powerful engine + very little weight = massive acceleration!
5. Did we mention they go really, really fast?

Now, brilliantly arranged according to their country of origin (took us weeks to think that one up), we proudly present ten of the best supercars ever built.

Faster, Faster, Faster ... Power!

Bugatti Veyron

The Bugatti Veyron is not only faster than an F1 car – it's the fastest production car in the world. So who did Top Gear choose to put behind the wheel? None other than Captain Slow himself.

It's the **fastest**, most **powerful** and most **expensive** road car the world has ever seen.

James took the Veyron out on Volkswagen's top-secret test track in Germany to see how fast he could go. The track has a main straight that's just over 5 miles long, so even James couldn't fail to give it the beans down the straight. Dressed in helmet and race suit, he climbed in and slotted a special key into the Bugatti to allow it to go stupidly fast. The car then hunkered down, ready to be as aerodynamic as possible. It looked good. Real good.

Even the door mirrors are designed to give downforce and help stop the car from taking off!

In profile

Despite massive cooling ducts, and no engine cover, the Veyron still has ten radiators all desperately trying to keep the massive engine cool. With this engine you could let an F1 car reach 120mph before you even set off – and you'd still beat it to 200mph!

It's got more radiators than my **house**.

BUGATTI

Check out that huge spoiler – it pushes the car down and gives it grip going round corners.

The carbon ceramic brakes give it incredible stopping power, too. You can go from 250mph to stand still in just 10 seconds. But it would take almost half a mile to stop as well!

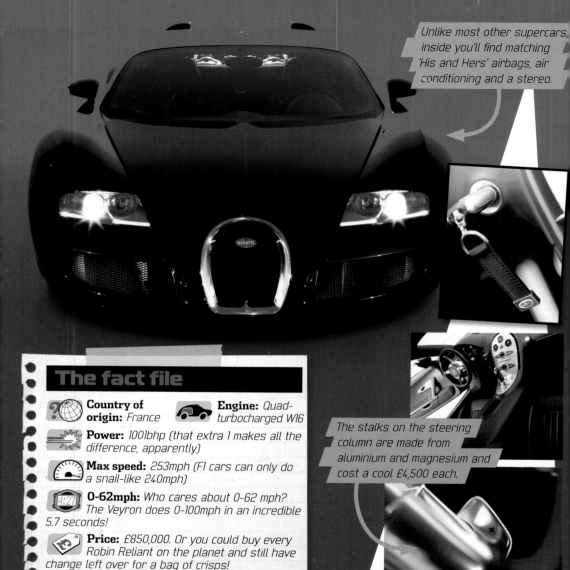

Unlike most other supercars, inside you'll find matching 'His and Hers' airbags, air conditioning and a stereo.

The stalks on the steering column are made from aluminium and magnesium and cost a cool £4,500 each.

The fact file

Country of origin: France

Engine: Quad-turbocharged W16

Power: 1001bhp (that extra 1 makes all the difference, apparently)

Max speed: 253mph (F1 cars can only do a snail-like 240mph)

0-62mph: Who cares about 0-62 mph? The Veyron does 0-100mph in an incredible 5.7 seconds!

Price: £850,000. Or you could buy every Robin Reliant on the planet and still have change left over for a bag of crisps!

Gadgets: You have to insert a special key in a slot by the door that makes the spoiler retract and the whole car 'hunkers down' to make it even more aerodynamic.

Cool stuff: At top speed, the Veyron covers the length of a football pitch every second!

This car is like **nothing** I've **ever** driven. It's like nothing I've ever **been in.** It's like nothing I even **sketched** as an eight-year-old in a maths book!

The power lap

Sadly, Bugatti haven't let our tame racing driver Le Stig borrow a Veyron yet. But if they did, maybe, just maybe, the Stig would be moved enough by the experience to speak.

The verdict

Jeremy took on Richard and James in a race across Europe. They were in a plane, he was in the Bugatti. The car won. Jeremy was pleased. Richard and James were not. Each car actually cost about £5 million to make, so VW (who own Bugatti) make a loss on every one. They made the car as a 'technical exercise' just to see if it could be done. And we're pleased to say, it could!

The Veyron is about doing things that people said were **just not possible.**

Porsche Carrera GT

Built from a mixture of titanium, magnesium and aluminium, the GT's incredibly light.

When a car is based exclusively on race technology, it's bound to be a bit special. When that technology also happens to belong to Porsche, then expect something incredible!

And that's exactly what the Germans have come up with in the Carrera GT. It's a Bavarian Beast with an almighty roar that's guaranteed to get the adrenalin pumping.

In profile

Design-wise, you could never mistake the beautifully rounded shape of a Porsche for anything else.

There's nothing fussy about this car. All the effort has gone into the monster engine and tip-top Teutonic technology. There's no spacious boot and deep shag pile carpets here. The Carrera GT is all about power. What Jeremy really loves about the Carrera GT is that it never seems to want to stop!

The **engine** was originally designed for racing but then Porsche had the bright idea of putting it in a road car. And the effect is absolutely **mind-blowing.**

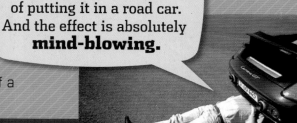

There are enough dials and knobs to keep you interested, from a top-notch stereo to the latest sat nav.

It may lack the flair of Italian cars but every **piece**, every **detail**, is as precise and as perfect as Germany's rail timetable.

Those huge air inlets are designed to help cool the engine.

Make a mistake and it **bites your head off**. It's that simple.

The fact file

Country of origin: Germany

Engine: V10

Power: 612bhp

Max speed: 205mph

0-62mph: 3.9 seconds

Price: £300,000. Not keen? OK, for the same money why not buy another German 'masterpiece'? Yep, you could own a classic 1970s VW Beetle. In fact, you could own 50.

Gadgets: Although more a necessity than a gadget, Porsche are particularly proud of their extra-strong, super-efficient carbon-ceramic brakes.

Cool stuff: The car's based on a model that won the Le Mans 24-Hour Race in 1998. This is an endurance race where three drivers take turns driving for 24 hours straight. Even Jeremy, Richard and James have given it a go. With a bit of help from the Stig.

The power lap

Eventually, His Holiness The Stig managed 1min 19.8sec. We say eventually because even Top Gear's tame racing driver had trouble controlling this one!

Lap Times

CARRERA GT. 1.98

McMERC 1.20.9

FERRARI 360CS .122.3

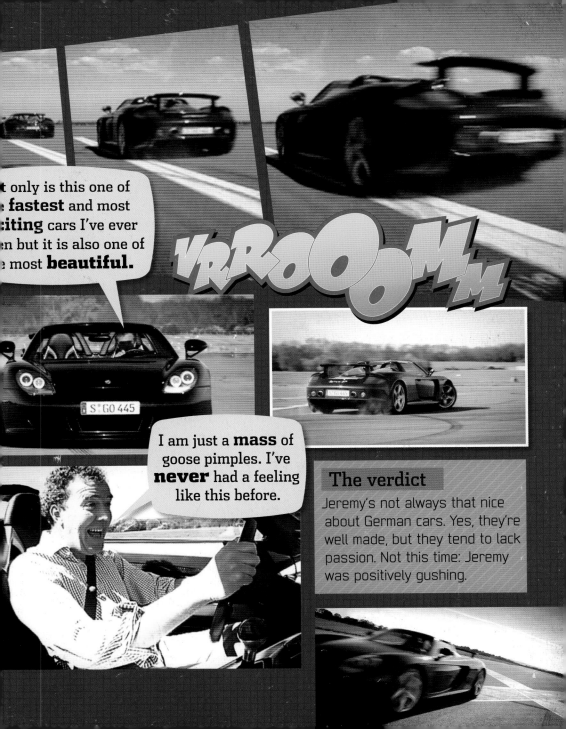

Maserati MC12

Jeremy has always loved Maseratis. Many (many!) years ago when he was just a lad, a beautiful picture of a glistening red Maserati 3500 GT jumped out from the pages of his Ladybird book of cars.

It was so much more exciting, so much more fun than the other big, grey cars that cluttered up the pages. But since the 1960s, Maserati has failed to come up with a car that's really got Jezza going. Would the MC12 be any different?

In profile

This is a big car. In fact, it's a huge car. It's a stretch-tastic 17ft long and 7ft wide, which doesn't make it a great choice for the weekly supermarket shop!

The tyres are massive, too, but because it's got a carbon fibre skeleton, it's still quite light. And that's pretty handy when you're trying to send the speedo spinning over the 200mph mark. This car oozes power. But look under the bonnet and you'll basically find a Ferrari Enzo. With power comes gas-guzzling and it only does about 5 miles per gallon.

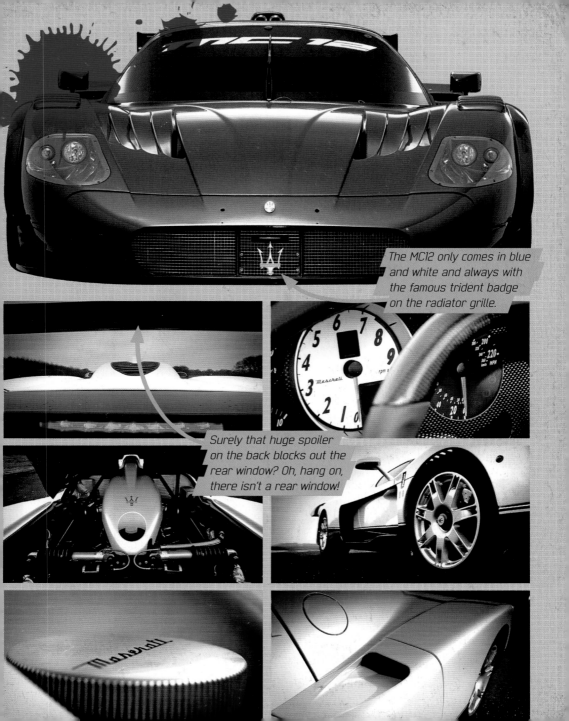

The MC12 only comes in blue and white and always with the famous trident badge on the radiator grille.

Surely that huge spoiler on the back blocks out the rear window? Oh, hang on, there isn't a rear window!

That's **so** quick... what a **bonkers** car!

The Fact File

 Country of origin: *Italy*

 Engine: *V12*

 Power: *630bhp*

 Max speed: *208mph*

 0-62mph: *3.8 seconds*

 Price: *A cool £412,000 – or put another way, that's about 50 loveable little Ford Fiestas.*

Gadgets: *Those thoughtful boffins at Maserati have added a special control that raises the nose to let you get over speed bumps.*

Cool stuff: *Only 50 MC12s have been made, which isn't surprising given the price tag. A special material called Brightex was used for the car's interior. And it's so expensive that even the mega-rich fashion industry can't afford to use it!*

The power lap

Lord Stig of Speedshire took the Maserati round the track in an astonishing 1min 18.9sec, which makes it one of the fastest cars ever on the show.

The new **fastest** car and you **didn't** like it?!

Well, speed isn' **everything**. I can't believe just said that!

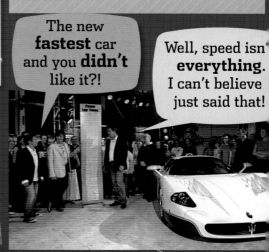

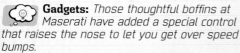

The verdict

Let's be honest, Jeremy just couldn't fall in love with this one. It's easy to be seduced by the speed but don't be because this car has a few problems. The price tag. The size. The price tag....

It's one of the most **difficult** and **twitchy** cars I've ever driven.

SKREEEEEEEEEEE

Far too big. **Far** too ugly.

We think Jeremy was talking about the car!

Ferrari Enzo

Ferrari only does fast. Designed to be a road car, it's really an F1 car in disguise. And this car's such a snorter that Jeremy was nearly lost for words. Nearly!

In profile

It's easy to see that Ferrari have used a lot of their F1 know-how to build the Enzo. You change gear by pulling forward a paddle on the steer column just like an F1 car – and it makes the change in just 150 milliseconds! There are no electric windows. No sat nav. There's nothing to distract you from the job of driving because when you are in here, that's all you want to do. Only astronauts have felt power like this before.

You only have to **look** at the F1-style steering wheel to know that you are in something that's **special** – it's a saucer full of secrets!

The monster making this torrent of sound is a V12.

I've **never known** such savagery. The **incredible** gear change and the **responsiveness** of the steering. And then there's the **speed** of the thing.

Mummy!

RRMMMBLL

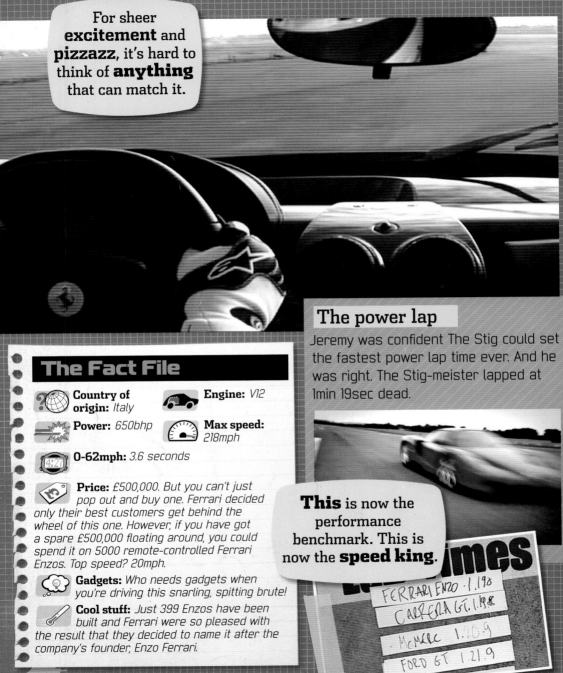

For sheer **excitement** and **pizzazz**, it's hard to think of **anything** that can match it.

The power lap

Jeremy was confident The Stig could set the fastest power lap time ever. And he was right. The Stig-meister lapped at 1min 19sec dead.

This is now the performance benchmark. This is now the **speed king**.

The Fact File

Country of origin: *Italy*

Engine: *V12*

Power: *650bhp*

Max speed: *218mph*

0-62mph: *3.6 seconds*

Price: *£500,000. But you can't just pop out and buy one. Ferrari decided only their best customers get behind the wheel of this one. However, if you have got a spare £500,000 floating around, you could spend it on 5000 remote-controlled Ferrari Enzos. Top speed? 20mph.*

Gadgets: *Who needs gadgets when you're driving this snarling, spitting brute!*

Cool stuff: *Just 399 Enzos have been built and Ferrari were so pleased with the result that they decided to name it after the company's founder, Enzo Ferrari.*

FERRARI ENZO · 1.19.8

CARRERA GT. 1.19.8

McMERC 1.20.9

FORD GT. 1.21.9

This is the division between **ordinary** and absolute **extraordinary.**

The verdict

Words couldn't describe how Jeremy felt about this car. And he tried many. Let's just say that the Enzo certainly got the Clarkson seal of approval.

Lamborghini Reventon

The dashboard is a thin, liquid crystal display and looks more like the instrument panel in a cockpit. Flick a switch and it changes to a slightly more recognizable 'car mode'.

Is this the most outrageous supercar ever? Probably. Inspired by a stealth fighter and looking more at home on the set of a sci-fi movie than out on the open road, it certainly had Jeremy and Richard drooling.

Even the tail lights are futuristic. They're made from LED lights in the shape of arrows.

And surely that must be the biggest exhaust pipe ever?

In profile

The inspiration for this car is F22 Raptor fighter. The car is basically a Lamborghini Murcielago with a futuristic new body. Oh, and the most powerful Lamborghini engine ever built.

The bodywork is a mixture of weird lines and angles. It looks like it could have been made in some bizarre carbon fibre origami session.

There are no spoilers to ruin that aerodynamic shape, just lots of special features that stop it taking off, like side pods and vents.

The matte finish is a first for a supercar. Although it's made from carbon fibre, it's painted to look like it's been cut out of solid granite!

The wheels have carbon fibre fins on them that brilliantly suck in cool air to stop the brakes from overheating.

The fact file

 Country of origin: *Italy*

 Engine: *V12*

 Power: *650bhp*

 Max speed: *212mph*

 0-62mph: *3.4 seconds*

 Price: *An astronomical £800,000. For that kind of money you could actually reserve eight seats on Virgin Galactic's first planned space flight!*

 Gadgets: *The Reventon has its own G-Force meter.*

Cool stuff: *According to Lamborghini tradition, the car is named after a Spanish fighting bull. The name of this model means 'explosion' or 'burst'.*

The power lap

With a price tag close to £1 million, not even good old Stiggy has been let near this one. Yet.

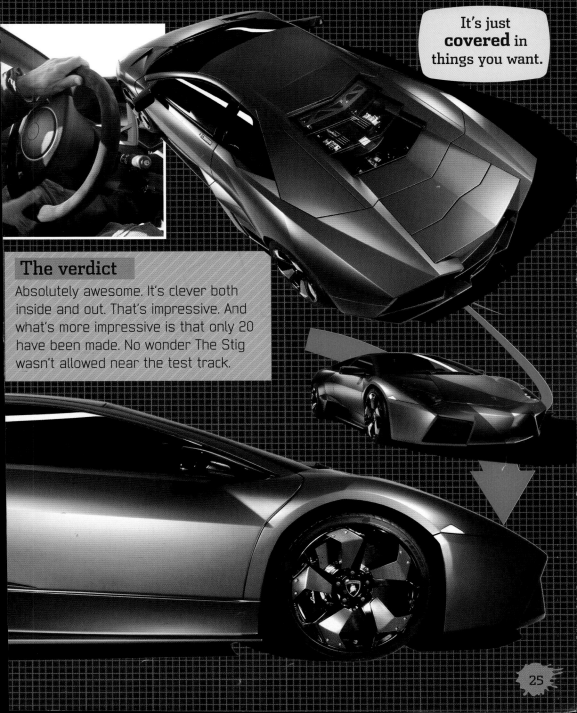

It's just **covered** in things you want.

The verdict

Absolutely awesome. It's clever both inside and out. That's impressive. And what's more impressive is that only 20 have been made. No wonder The Stig wasn't allowed near the test track.

Ford GT

The Ford GT was built to celebrate Ford's 100th birthday. Its inspiration was the GT40, a truly remarkable car that took on Ferrari in the 1960s, and won Le Mans four times in a row. And that's something that Jeremy remembers well from when he was a kid.

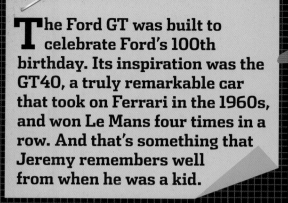

> The acceleration is **astonishing.** It actually hurts your neck muscles.

In profile

Ford wanted this GT to be more than just a pretty face. But despite all the hype, they pinched the engine straight from under the bonnet of their own Lightning pick-up truck! The GT engine is extra special though because it's built by hand. You can see it through the back window as you drive. But when Jeremy opened it up to take a look at the pistons, he was overcome.

> Look at **that!** Look at it! It makes me feel six years old all over again. In fact, I think I've **wet** myself.

The old GT40 had one flaw: the roof was too low for Jeremy to fit his head inside!

Those enormous tyres also help keep it on course.

The Americans have never built a truly fast car that can also go round corners. Until now!

I **love** this thing. I love it **more** than I thought I was going to.

The power lap

A disappointing 1min 21.9sec. But at least our resident speed merchant The Stig didn't run out of petrol, which is more than you can say for Jeremy who ended up on empty during his test drive!

The fact file

 Country of origin: USA

 Engine: V8 supercharged

 Power: 500bhp

 Max speed: 212mph

 0-62mph: 4 seconds

 Price: £111,000. A bargain when you look at the price of a Maserati or a Porsche.

 Gadgets: Nothing special, but rumour has it, Ford are considering making a five-seater hatchback version, with a tow bar for a caravan. Jeremy, Richard and James will take one each!

 Cool stuff: Those fantastic racing stripes and also the brilliant doors. Open them and half the roof comes away, too.

As far as handling and grip are concerned, it's **epic!**

I don't think I'll **ever** want to get out of it.

From every **angle** you can see its muscle car biceps straining to **burst** out of the bodywork.

The verdict

The Americans only sent 28 Ford GTs to the UK. And guess who got one of them? That's right. Jeremy. Would he turn down one of the fastest production cars that is also 'reasonably' priced? We think not. It must be love.

I'm running out of **runway!**

Ariel Atom

Forget your huge car factories in Italy or multi-nationals in the US, the Atom is very much a British affair. It's built by Ariel, a small but perfectly formed company in that hotbed of car manufacturing... Somerset. There are just seven employees making 30 cars a year. And if Mrs Clarkson would let him, Jeremy would buy every one!

Top Gear magazine took the Atom to the frozen north and found out too late it doesn't have a heater.

www.arielmotor.co.uk

In profile

This car really is little more than an engine, a chassis, four wheels and a seat. The engine and gearbox come courtesy of Honda, while the bodywork looks like a few scaffolding poles welded together.

The chassis forms a skeleton on the outside of the car and there's virtually no bodywork, which makes the car incredibly light.

And it's this power-to-weight ratio that gives the car such massive acceleration. In fact, kilo for kilo, it's got more beans than a Ferrari Enzo.

This is driving **Nirvana.**

on't drive this car earing a wig – that's e air intake straight ehind the driver's head!

have **never** ever iven anything that celerates so **fast!**

The power lap

Our captive nuclear processor The Stig lapped at a rip-roaring 1min 19.5sec. Jeremy also took on a Honda motorbike round the track – and thrashed it. The bike just couldn't keep up and the Atom won by a massive 4 seconds.

And away he goes like a **rocket!**

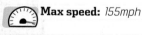

EEEEEYOOWWWWW

It's so quick it can destroy your entire face!

The fact file

 Country of origin: *England*

 Engine: *Super-charged Honda Civic Type-R K20*

 Power: *300bhp*

 Max speed: *155mph*

 0-62mph: *If you can change gear fast enough it will do it in 2.9 seconds!*

 Price: *Under £35,000. Or roughly the same price as a new, top-of-the-range Renault Espace people carrier. Now, which would you rather be dropped off at school in?*

Gadgets: *A car that's got no windscreen and virtually no bodywork is hardly going to be big on gadgets, is it?*

 Cool stuff: *As you're driving you can actually see the mechanical parts moving.*

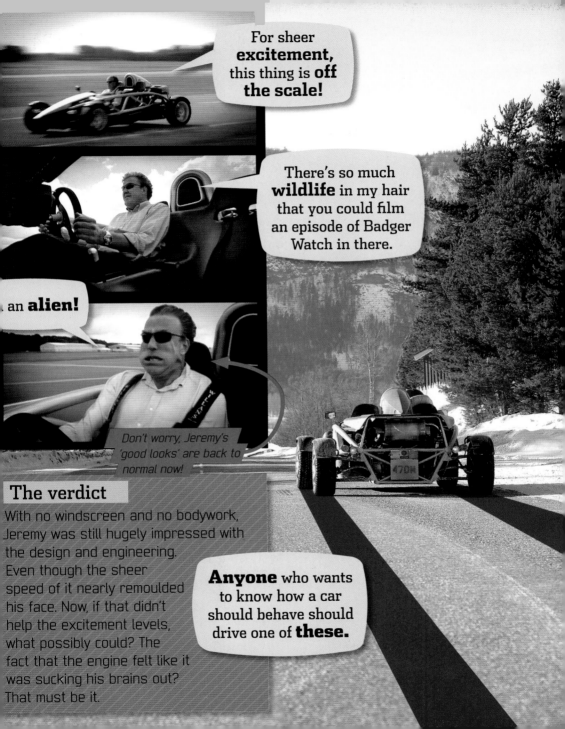

For sheer **excitement**, this thing is **off the scale!**

There's so much **wildlife** in my hair that you could film an episode of Badger Watch in there.

an **alien!**

Don't worry, Jeremy's 'good looks' are back to normal now!

The verdict

With no windscreen and no bodywork, Jeremy was still hugely impressed with the design and engineering. Even though the sheer speed of it nearly remoulded his face. Now, if that didn't help the excitement levels, what possibly could? The fact that the engine felt like it was sucking his brains out? That must be it.

Anyone who wants to know how a car should behave should drive one of **these.**

Mercedes McLaren SLR

Under that long, noble front end roars a great engine.

You can't help but love those gullwing doors.

This supercar is hand-built at McLaren's state-of-the-art technology centre in deepest, darkest Woking. SLR stands for 'super-light racing' and is taken from some famous Mercedes models of the 1950s. It's a pretty good description of the McLaren SLR because even though it's a big car, the company's technical wizards have made the whole body out of carbon fibre. And while it may be three times as expensive as steel, it's much stronger and much, much lighter.

That's **extraordinary** – all the organs in my body that were pushed to the back when I accelerated have now shot **forward.** And my tonsils are now in front of my teeth.

And in case you need a bit of extra help, there's a rear air brake that flips up too.

In profile

Surprisingly for a supercar, it comes with an automatic gearbox. But then again it can now claim to be the fastest automatic car in the world!

Now, Jeremy isn't someone who usually gets that excited about a car's brakes. But the McLaren SLR's are a bit special. They're made from silicon carbide with a ceramic coating and only ever used in super high performance vehicles (they're also known as supercars, funnily enough). Jeremy decided to test them by stopping the car while doing 120mph. But he only gave himself the distance to do it in that the Highway Code suggests when doing 60mph.

And he succeeded...

... but look at those brakes!

The power lap

His Royal Stigness liked this one, taking it round in 1min 20.9sec.

This is a **fantastic** car. It's a grippy, agile, adrenalin rush.

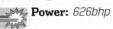
The Fact File

 Country of origin: *England*

 Engine: *V8 super-charged*

 Power: *626bhp*

 Max speed: *208mph*

0-62mph: *3.8seconds*

Price: *If you don't fancy paying £312,000 then you could buy 180km of Scaletrix track and two McLaren F1 cars to race on it! And that's enough track to go round Silverstone 36 times!*

Gadgets: *Got car problems? Press the spanner button on the car phone, and you'll be put straight through to the mechanics at the factory where it was built.*

Cool stuff: *The glowing ceramic brakes are a nice touch but there's nothing compared to the starter button. It's hidden underneath a special flap on top of the gearstick, so you can flick it, then feel the 'power'!*

Lap Times

McMerc 1.20.9
MURCIELAGO 123.7
ZONDA 123.8
NNIDEGGOENNNISSSOEUGGOOUE

KA-POWWW

The verdict

A car that is the fastest automatic car in the world with the most impressive brakes Jeremy has ever experienced. He thought he'd discovered a supercar that you really could use everyday.

Even though it's so **aggressive,** it's as civilised as **Switzerland** and no harder to handle than a **vacuum cleaner.**

Supercar innards with supermarket convenience. It's like making an exquisite **soufflé** and then garnishing it... with a slab of **lard.**

Aston Martin DBS

The Aston Martin chaps like to describe this car having as much character as James Bond. That's a big call. It apparently is the perfect blend of Aston's road cars and track cars to produce a pure thoroughbred. But, try as he might, Jeremy just didn't get that thoroughbred feeling.

There's adaptive suspension that you can activate to let it know if it's on a track or on a road.

When driving around the Top Gear test track, Jeremy appreciated the simple features like the steering and the brakes, especially when enjoying doing a few power slides. But he just didn't feel sheer terror and that's what supposed to make a supercar a supercar, right?

In profile

The DBS is unlike other supercars – it's not only hugely powerful, but practical, too. It's got a boot. And lots of storage space behind the driver. The engine is at the front and is even rather reliable.

I **like** the steering. I do like that. And I **like** the brakes.

The tyres were especially designed for the DBS by Pirelli.

It's not a **thoroughbred.** Perhaps then, it's a work of **art.**

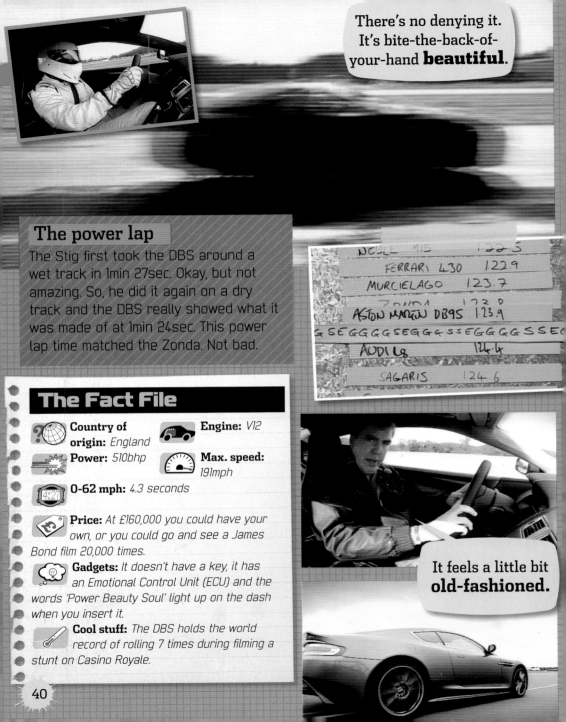

There's no denying it. It's bite-the-back-of-your-hand **beautiful**.

The power lap

The Stig first took the DBS around a wet track in 1min 27sec. Okay, but not amazing. So, he did it again on a dry track and the DBS really showed what it was made of at 1min 24sec. This power lap time matched the Zonda. Not bad.

NOBLE   M15   133.5
FERRARI 430   122.9
MURCIELAGO   123.7
ZONDA   123.0
ASTON MARTIN DB9S   123.9
G SE GG G G SE GG G SS E GG G G SS E C
AUDI L8   124.4
SAGARIS   124.6

The Fact File

Country of origin: England

Engine: V12

Power: 510bhp

Max. speed: 191mph

0-62 mph: 4.3 seconds

Price: At £160,000 you could have your own, or you could go and see a James Bond film 20,000 times.

Gadgets: It doesn't have a key, it has an Emotional Control Unit (ECU) and the words 'Power Beauty Soul' light up on the dash when you insert it.

Cool stuff: The DBS holds the world record of rolling 7 times during filming a stunt on Casino Royale.

It feels a little bit **old-fashioned.**

This is James Bond's **actual** car from the movie (before he crashed it)

TT=378-20

SKREEEEEEEEEEE

Whoops!

The verdict

Jeremy wasn't scared out of his mind when driving the DBS but he was impressed. The performance and comfort makes it the perfect car for driving holidays with Mrs Clarkson to the south of France. How very English.

Koenigeggseggeggsegg CCX

Mostly the **oomph** comes from under the bonnet.

The first time Jeremy drove a Koenigsegg it proved so fast the Top Gear camera crew couldn't actually follow it! They were better prepared second time around, although at times Jeremy did look genuinely terrified as he tore down the track.

When you lift off, huge jets of flame shoot out of the exhaust as unburnt fuel is ignited by the heat of the pipes.

In profile

Sleek, silver and smooth, the Koenigsegg is designed to be as aerodynamic as a fish. There are no silly sticky-out bits like spoilers to get in the way, or keep it on the ground. This car is seriously fast. It's also made of carbon fibre which means it weighs next to nothing.

No point worrying what's behind you, as the rear window is little more than a porthole.

It sounds like a Norse god of **thunder** gargling with a **hammer**.

The fact file

 Country of origin: *Sweden*

 Max speed: *250mph*

 Engine: *Twin supercharged V8*

 0-62mph: *3.2seconds*

 Power: *800bhp. But if you tune it to run on eco-friendly biofuel, you get more than 900bhp.*

 Price: *£415,000. Or you could invest in another Scandinavian icon, a 'Baren' toilet brush set from Ikea. In fact, you could invest in 83,000 of them!*

 Gadgets: *It's packed with controls straight out of a spaceship. There's even a radio but the engine's so loud Stig couldn't hear his favourite Meatloaf CD when he drove it.*

Cool stuff: *While taking part in the Gumball Rally in America, a Koenigsegg received the world's biggest speeding ticket. The cops clocked it at 242mph! Whoever said the Swedes were boring?*

The power lap

The fastest car that The Right Honourable Member for Fastville, The Stig, had ever driven around the track, with an astonishing time of 1min 17.6sec. That's after some of Top Gear's own little modifications. He did manage to spin the Koenigsegg first time he took it out. But that just annoyed him so he stuck on a back spoiler to give the car more downforce and then ripped up the tarmac at a blistering pace.

POWER LAP TIMES

1SSEGG(SE(NIGNIG)SE(LI(ISEG(CX2 WITH THE TOP GEAR WING 1:17.6

ZONDA F	1:18.4
MASERATI MC12	1:18.9
FERRARI ENZO	1:19.0
ATOM	1:19.5
CARRERA GT	1:19.8

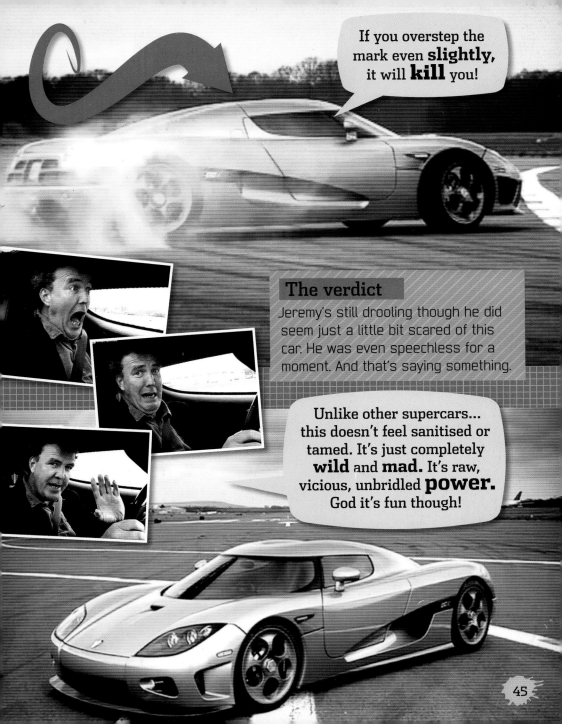

If you overstep the mark even **slightly,** it will **kill** you!

The verdict

Jeremy's still drooling though he did seem just a little bit scared of this car. He was even speechless for a moment. And that's saying something.

Unlike other supercars... this doesn't feel sanitised or tamed. It's just completely **wild** and **mad.** It's raw, vicious, unbridled **power.** God it's fun though!

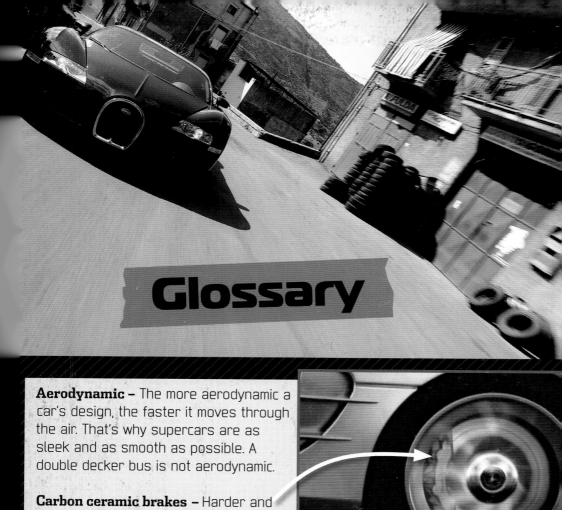

Glossary

Aerodynamic – The more aerodynamic a car's design, the faster it moves through the air. That's why supercars are as sleek and as smooth as possible. A double decker bus is not aerodynamic.

Carbon ceramic brakes – Harder and less likely to melt than traditional steel brake discs. A handy addition to any car, even if they do have a tendency to glow when hot.

Carbon fibre – Very expensive material often used on the bodywork of a supercar. It contains strands of carbon which make it very strong and very light.

Chassis – This is a car's skeleton that supports all the moving bits. Most are hidden under the bodywork, except the Ariel Atom, which flaunts it on the outside.

Child seat – Not sure how this got here but unlikely to ever be found in a supercar.

Downforce – Because supercars go so fast, and are often quite light, they need spoilers and wings to create downforce which presses the car down, giving it more grip on the road.

Flappy paddle transmission – Clunking through the gears is now a thing of the past! Using stupidly high-tech computer, ahh stuff, it now means you can change gears ridiculously fast.

Flat battery – Very annoying. Means the car won't start. Even more annoying if you've paid £500,000 for the car.

G-force – The G stands for gravity, a strange invisible force that pins you to the seat when you accelerate. Or makes you feel sick when cornering at 200 mph.

GT – Stands for Grand Tourer and means the car's designers have combined comfort and luxury with speed. The sort of car you can drive without getting a numb bum after five minutes.

Gullwing doors – Mad doors that have the hinge on the top rather than the side. They're not just for show though and do actually make it easier to get in and out of the car.

in the midsts of time with the Rolls Royce Silver Ghost of 1921. Today you can spot a supercar because it looks different, it sounds different and it goes like the absolute clappers.

LED (light emitting diode) – Nifty little lights that could soon send the traditional light bulb the same way as the Dodo. They light up much more quickly and are great as brake lights because the harder you push the brake pedal the brighter they shine. Check out the indicator lights on the Reventon.

Rear mid-engine (RMR) – Unlike Dad's runaround, many, but not all, supercars have the engine at the back. It helps make the car more stable but can make the cabin very noisy.

Spoilers – These are sticky-out bits on the backs of cars. They look silly on a Ford Fiesta but magnificent on a supercar, where they push against the air rushing past and make the car press down on the road more.

Supercar – Some say the first supercar was the Lamborghini Miura from the mid-1960s, others say that it began way back

Supercharger – A clever little device that boosts the power of a car's engine. Obviously, all supercars should have a supercharger. Or a turbocharger.

Turbocharger – Another clever little device that boosts the power of a car's engine. Both devices force more air into the engine cylinders to produce more power. Petrol + more air = more bang!

V8, V12 etc – The way in which a car's cylinders are arranged in a V formation around the engine, with an equal number of each side. Inside each cylinder is a piston which produces all the power.